Kick Back, Lie Down and Put my Feet up

Debbie Bolton

BookLeaf Publishing

Presentation by *BookLeaf Publishing*

Web: www.bookleafpub.com

E-mail: info@bookleafpub.com

ISBN: 9789357440349

First edition 2023

I dedicate this book to Steve, my husband of 14+ years. Without your support, I would not have the space to be able to achieve everything I do. This is my ode to you, my whispering herald.

ACKNOWLEDGEMENT

I would like to thank BookLeaf Publishing for the opportunity to write these poems and have them printed.

A huge Thank you to my husband Steve who has been my muse for this book. He loves the idea of it and denies nothing! Thank you for your support, fun and smiles through this all.

PREFACE

Thank you for purchasing my book. I wrote this book to show a fun insight into the life of a married couple. It is a bit of fun and you may identify with some of the situations that I write about – both good and bad.

I am writing this from the viewpoint of my husband and in his voice, but this is what I imagine is going on in his mind with real life thrown in. He has a habit of kicking back, lying down and putting his feet up on the sofa, hence the title of the book. He calls it relaxation, I call it an annoyance and a position that he stubbornly wants to stay in. Whichever side of the coin you come down on, have a read and enjoy the tales.

The Annoying Friend

I am in a shop with my wife and my friend calls,
He wants to fix his car.
He is and annoying friend.
He consistently wants to do everything at last minute,
It often breaks into my plans.
I want to be at home so I can...kick back, lie down and put my feet up.

It is New Years Eve and neither my wife or myself are happy about it.
He was at the house the night before,
He was encroaching on our time with our niece.
I want an excuse not to see him.
So I suggest we spend our New Year celebrations with her brother's family.
She agrees, I am happy.
Later, I can...kick back, lie down and put my feet up.

We are heading home and I want to see my friend.
I ask what we are doing until we see her brother.
She wants to tie up the year with her goals and reaffirm other goals she has set.

She wants to be able to spend a little bit of time in her office.
I suggest that since she will be busy, I will not be missed, so I can now go to my friend's house.
I head out so I can...kick back, lie down and put my feet up.

My brother from another mother calls to inform me that he is home and will come and pick us up.
I tell him I am not at home but my wife is and to call her to collect her.
We agree that he will collect me later.
I continue to spend time with my friend and look forward to seeing my niece and family,
Because then I can...kick back, lie down and put my feet up.

I am called to be told my niece is nearing going to bed.
My niece tells me to come home now.
I tell them that I am getting into the car now and heading home.
They sound happy, I feel worthy to...kick back, lie down and put my feet up.

I am called again.
My niece asks where I am and I tell her that I am leaving right now.

Everyone is sounding a little agitated that I am not there.
I may need to earn my right again to...kick back, lie down and put my feet up.

An hour later, I call my bro to be picked up.
When he collects me, he is wrapped up warm.
I arrive and my niece runs up and hugs me.
She is happy to see me.
She is the only one that is happy.
I will need to put some effort into being allowed to...kick back, lie down and put my feet up.

My wife is grumpy.
She is really grumpy.
I sit on the sofa and tell the tale of the headlight that needed to be changed.
I move onto the tale of the shed that needs organised.
She does not look impressed,
I am going to have to work hard to be able to...kick back, lie down and put my feet up.

My wife sits on the sofa with her arms crossed.
I go over and sit down beside her.
I place my arm around her.
I am trying to convey the message, "I am sorry, I am here now."

Maybe, soon, I can...kick back, lie down and put my feet up.

I know I have messed up.
I know how to make it up to her with one small gesture.
She has now forgiven me.
It is now time to...kick back, lie down and put my feet up.

My Wife

My wife is back to work today when everyone is
still off for the winter holidays.
She has received a bit of hassle from one of her
clients.
She has been up early and completed her entire
to do list.
I do not understand the depths of what she
actually does.
She needs to take a leaf out of my book, I
would...kick back, lie down and put feet up.

After further investigation, I have found out she
has been awake since 4am.
She is home earlier than expected.
I encourage my laziness when she says that she
is practising her art skills.
I watch her fill her sketch book with charcoal.
This is the best time to...kick back, lie down and
put my feet up.

Time has passed and she is disappointed with
her attempt at a tin.
I tell her that all she needs to do is have a bit
more practice.
She appears content with my response.

Knowing that I am a good husband and able to give worthy praise,
I continue to...kick back, lie down and put my feet up.

The Bathroom Incident

We just got back from the in laws.
I have eaten copious amounts of fine food.
I have discussed games with the gaming contingent, work with the working contingent and lego with the lego fans.
I have helped out with the meal by taking plates to and from the table.
I have given my young niece a lot of attention, playing with planes, dinosaurs and using our imaginations.
I have had a satisfying day.
I need to...kick back, lie down and put my feet up.

I decide that my actions need to be rewarded by participating in one of my favourite activities,
I sit in the bathroom watching videos on my phone.
After a short while, my wife interrupts me, knocking on the door and declaring that she needs to use the bathroom as she is about to go to bed.
I have forgotten that she gets up early to work on her soul goals.

Luckily, I was finished 25 minutes ago, I have just been watching a stream of a game.
I finish up and smile at her as I depart the bathroom.
It must be time to...kick back, lie down and put my feet up.

She does not look amused.
After further investigation, she has been waiting to brush her teeth and put on whatever face cream she uses at night.
She has also given up her reading time and instead, done housework just to wait for me to exit the bathroom.
She is not pleased.
This is not the time to...kick back, lie down and put my feet up.

I try to save the situation by offering to put on more washing,
But she has already done that.
I try to save the day again by saying I will finish the dishes,
She says, "thank you."
I have regained my hero status.
I wait five minutes and head upstairs to tuck her into bed.
She is lying on top of the bed with all the duvets off of her.

Abnormally, she is physically very hot tonight.
No need for me to tuck her night.
It might be time for me to...kick back, lie down and put my feet up.

I bid her goodnight and head downstairs to watch TV.
I contemplate what a good husband I actually am whilst I...kick back, lie down and put my feet up.

The Alcove

My wife has announced that it is time to tidy the alcove in the living room.
I really don't want to.
I want to continue in my favourite position on the sofa.
I ask her, with a huge exclamation, why does she want to do it.
She referred to a conversation we had that morning about doing it now.
She reminds me that I agreed.
I must have been ignoring her again and agreed to get her to stop talking.
I want to remain..kicked back, laid down with my feet up.

I try to delay her by suggesting that is supposed to be on a phone call.
She tells me the other person has cancelled.
After many protestations, I finally move as I see she has started without me.
I want to maintain being...kicked back, laid down with my feet up.

She is getting excited by this tidying up and reorganising malarkey.

She has now started to declutter.
She has moved from the alcove to the cupboard under the alcove.
Now the space in front of the alcove and a glass set of shelving.
Please woman, I just want to...kick back, lie down and put my feet up.

I think she is overdoing it but she is moving everything about.
She is like a light gazelle enjoying the freedom of running around.
I don't understand how she does it, she has been awake since 4am.
I look at my space on the sofa,
I am sure it is calling me to...kick back, lie down and put my feet up.

Then slowly, she is tiring out and talking about going to bed soon.
This is good news.
This is great news!
She goes off to bed.
There is one final thing I need to do for the evening...kick back, lie down and put my feet up.

Waiting For My Bro

It is the last day of my holiday before starting work,
I want to do something to mark the end of it.
I want to enjoy myself, so I organise spending time with my wife's brother.
He likes a laugh and we play the same online games.
With him, I can...kick back, lie down and put my feet up.

My wife's company does not let people off during seasonal times,
Her last time off was over six months ago.
She has just finished another day at work and brought home boxes for her Dad.
He moves house next month.
That will be a day when I can not...kick back, lie down and put my feet up.

We fill his car and I feel a real sense of achievement today.
I have managed to help him by completely filling his car.
She is offering to make me food, I decline.

I know I will get something better than eggs
from my bro.
Then I can...kick back, lie down and put my feet
up.

My wife is cold. She works in prolonged
coldness at work.
No matter how many thermal vests or layers she
puts on, she is always cold.
She is sitting next to the fire warming her hands.
She is talking about something, I just agree and
take no notice.
I want to be in the position of being...kicked
back, laid down with my feet up.

My bro messages me to say he is on his way.
I have five minutes. I could get up and make her
a cup of tea,
But I have only been up an hour and I have
moved boxes into a car.
Instead...I kick back, lie down and put my feet
up.

When I Am Comfortable In My Favourite Position

I woke up late, it is my day off.
I have managed to watch a few YouTube videos, make some lunch.
I eat it and then I...kick back, lie down and put my feet up.

My wife says something,
I am not concentrating,
I try to remember at least one word, I can't.
I apologise and ask her to repeat it.
It is nothing that will bother me now, I say I will do it later.
Then I continue to...kick back, lie down and put my feet up.

My wife is doing the dishes,
I can hear the clinking of the china.
I still have my plate and cup in front of me in the living room.
I consider getting up and taking them through.
I am far too comfortable, so I proceed to...kick back, lie down and put my feet up.

I feel the beginnings of a full bladder.

The bathroom is on the same floor, it is only ten steps from this position.
I check in with my bladder,
I can wait another ten minutes.
I progress to...kick back, lie down and put my feet up.

My wife shouts my name,
I shout back, "yes".
I hear everything she says.
I respond, I know she can barely hear me at the best of times.
She thinks I have said something else. I could get up to tell her,
That would require effort.
So, I resume to...kick back, lie down and put my feet up.

My drink is sitting on the coffee table, I stretch and try to reach it, it is definitely not happening unless I move.
I wriggle around, I stretch again.
My cup is still out of reach, it will still be warm in a few minutes.
I look longingly at the cup whilst I...kick back, lie down and put my feet up.

I found a solution to my drink out of reach problem.

I have my glass on a footstool beside the sofa.
It is within arms reach.
I chug a few mouthfuls so I can continue
to...kick back, lie down and put my feet up.

I see it is not raining outside, the grass needs cut.
I think about getting the lawn mower out.
I contemplate my wife smiling and thanking me.
Instead, I remain...kicked back, laid down with
my feet up.

Pick Up After Work

It is 4pm and I want to be finished work.
The colleague taking over my job arrives at the workstation two minutes before the hour.
She has questions. Many questions. I just want to be out of here.
She asks the same things over and over again.
I think of a time when I can...kick back, lie down and put my feet up.

I have finally managed to get away and I am 17 minutes past the hour.
There is nobody from my shift left in the building.
I can not see my bro or the trainee who I car share with.
That means only one thing, my wife is in the car park awaiting my arrival to the car.
I wish I could be at home so I can...kick back, lie down and put my feet up.

I get out to the corridor, look out the windows and my car is sitting with everyone in it.
I glimpse at my wife's face and she does not look amused.

I still need to get my bag out of my locker, use the facilities and clock out of my shift.
I assure her that I will not be long by placing up two fingers to tell her, I will be two minutes.
I can't wait to get home to...kick back, lie down and put my feet up.

My locker is being tricky and sucking me into a time vortex.
The bathroom pulls me into it, I have significant relief of being off my feet.
I enjoy the small respite.
I head back out with my bag and log out.
Now I am on the way home to...kick back, lie down and put my feet up.

I approach the car and my wife appears rather upset.
Strangely, she asks why I gave her the peace sign at the window.
I chuckle to myself and tell her that it was the sign for two minutes.
She tells me that they have waited seven minutes since seeing me last.
I wish I was at home to...kick back, lie down and put my feet up.

She stops the car outside the lab.

The car partakes in the obligatory departing enthusiastic wave to the working staff.
The staff wave back and all is well with the world,
That is, apart from my wife.
I need to be at home so I can...kick back, lie down and put my feet up.

I need to be able to soothe my wife who is acting like a savage beast.
She is tired from a week of working and 4am starts.
This feels like a task that I am going to struggle with,
I wish I could just...kick back, lie down and put my feet up.

Giving My Wife A Lay In

My wife has woken up to her own alarm and
asked me to switch off mine.
I tell her it is her alarm and she rolls over to
switch it off.
My own alarm rings five minutes later.
She does not make a sound.
She keeps snoozing.
In this moment, I could...kick back, lie down and
put my feet up.

She gets up so early every day,
Her body is telling her to sleep.
This is unusual for her, and I try not to wake her
every time I hit snooze.
Instead of switching on the big light, I click the
bedside sheep lamp on.
I can see what I am doing, she is still resting
with her eyes closed.
Oh, I could go downstairs and get in a
sneaky...kick back, lie down and put my feet up.

I am dressed and ready to leave the bedroom.
I make my way round to her side of the bed and
gently tell her that I am about to leave for work.

Selflessly, she asks if I want her to make a
coffee for me.
I tell her, “no” and to have a lie in and go back
to sleep.
I am totally winning best husband of the year
award.
I deserve to...kick back, lie down and put my
feet up.

She does not often sleep past 6am, so I am
pleased to urge her to rest.
She needs to get her life work balance back into
sync.
I feel accomplished in being able to be useful
and help my independent wife.
With this sense of achievement,
I wonder if I actually have time to...kick back,
lie down and put my feet up.

Finished Work For The Day

I have finished another day at work.
The normal people have annoyed me.
I have played my usual games on my gaming device during my break.
As I have left, I have completed the ritual of waving to people in the lab until they wave back at me.
Time to go home so I can...kick back, lie down and put my feet up.

I have car-shared and driven home the trainee and my bro.
I have got into the house and it appears empty.
I shout on my wife and she answers,
I deduce she is in her office.
Can I go straight to the sofa to...kick back, lie down and put my feet up.

She comes downstairs, greets me and starts to make dinner.
I take my time to shower and watch a few gaming videos.
By the time I get to the kitchen, she informs me that it is 38 seconds until cooking is over.
Perfect timing for dinner.

Soon I will...kick back, lie down and put my feet up.

She puts on a new series from a streaming service.
We eat dinner and I whole hearted approve of this program,
It is is full of intrigue, suspense, real life and science fiction.
I feel happy and contented with my day,
So there is only one thing left to do...kick back, lie down and put my feet up.

Midnight Movements

It is midnight and I have finished work.
I remember that my wife has been at art class,
So, the car is at home.
No biggie, I can walk the 13 minutes home.
Then I can...kick back, lie down and put my feet up.

My bro and trainee rely on me for a lift.
The trainee does not mind walking his 15 minutes home.
My bro definitely does not want to walk his 45 minutes home.
I offer him a lift if he walks home with me.
We talk, but I want to...kick back, lie down and put my feet up.

Our walk is more like 20 minutes,
He is not used to walking and the steepness of some of the inclines makes him puff.
I don't mind the walk.
It is the reason we moved so close to work.
I am thinking about the sofa so I can...kick back, lie down and put my feet up.

Whilst talking, he checks his phone for
something,
I check my phone and there is a message from
my wife.
She has reminded me it is bin day tomorrow and
to take it round to the front of the house.
Now I must delay the inevitable...kick back, lie
down and put my feet up.

I get home and take my bro to his house.
I get to the kitchen and find more recycling for
the bin.
I take it out.
Now I begin the negotiation of the bin to the
street.
I will soon...kick back, lie down and put my feet
up.

It is closer to 1am, I try to be quiet.
I open the first gate, pull the bin through,
Close the gate.
I must do the same again with the second gate.
I am looking forward to my time when I
can...kick back, lie down and put my feet up.

A light turns on in my next door neighbour's
house.
I stop for a moment, then fumble with the gate
as quietly as possible.

I tip toe down the path,
With the bin rumbling behind me.
I wish I could...kick back, lie down and put my feet up.

I am at the top of the two steps.
I take a deep breath.
I bump the bin down.
There are two large crashes as I do.
I am near to a time when I can...kick back, lie down and put my feet up.

I glance up at the neighbours house again,
The light is off.
I take another deep breath.
I continue the light treading motion as the bin continues its low rumble.
I am in sight of the moment when I can...kick back, lie down and put my feet up.

I finally have the bin in place.
I am sure I have woken up half the street.
Why does she always ask me to do the bin in the middle of the night?
I can't wait to get back in the house to...kick back, lie down and put my feet up.

The Coffee Shop Incident

I have been forced to go into the sunlight by my wife.
I have surprised myself that I have not burned to a crisp with my vampirism type sun avoidance.
She conned me into a coffee, I was bored whilst she wrote in her notebook, it is her version of playing with a phone at a table.
Can't wait to get home so I can...kick back, lie down and put my feet up.

I try to extend my day out to my advantage and ask for another coffee.
This has pushed her to investigation mode.
The waitress comes over, I order a just about unpronounceable amaretto cappuccino and sneak in a toffee delight tray bake.
I wish I was at home so I can...kick back, lie down and put my feet up.

This delicious snack is just what I need, I am trying to be posh by eating it with the fork and knife provided.
My wife is mocking me, so I pick it up with my man hands.
I wish I was at home to savour this.

I want to...kick back, lie down and put my feet up.

I want to go home, but she wants to go to a few more shops.
I am sure the sun is joining up all my freckles, I must get back inside.
She does not understand my pain of being out.
I want to...kick back, lie down and put my feet up.

My plan to leave the coffee shop has been foiled by seven elderly ladies all individually trying to pay for their afternoon jaunt out.
The pressure of being out is getting to me again, I get my handheld games console out to play a game.
I dream of a time when I can get home so I can...kick back, lie down and put my feet up.

Avoiding Housework

I have woken up to a message from my wife
asking if I am awake,
There has to be more to it than just checking up
on me.
I reply asking her, "what sup?"
She calls me to say to expect her father to pick
up boxes.
I am pleased with the prospect of claiming back
space in the house.
I already want to...kick back, lie down and put
my feet up.

He arrives within the hour with his new car
already rammed with boxes.
It turns out he has been to see my wife at work
and she has given him many, many boxes.
I am an expert of placing things in things.
He leaves with a car fuller than when he arrived.
I feel satisfied in being able to help.
So I muse about...kicking back, laying down and
putting my feet up.

My wife is home and I appear to be agitating her
with holding a conversation through the
bathroom door.

My day has been so much more diverse, and she is giving one word answers like I am disturbing her doing something important.
She makes herself a cup of tea and sits down to get warm.
Apparently she is cold from lack of heating at work again.
I suggest that she should...kick back, lie down and put her feet up.

She suggests making dinner and to tidy up a bit.
Her words always fill me with dread when I hear her mention 'tidy.'
This means that she will keep going until dinner is ready.
She will not stop.
How can I now justify my want of...kicking back, laying down and putting my feet up.

Normally, I would use the time to listen to music whilst doing dishes.
Sometimes, I will even stop and watch a video from start to finish.
Not her, she is focused, and expects me to help out in the jobs I don't like.
So, I do what every self respecting man does, I announce a visit to the bathroom.
This is second to...kicking back, lying down and putting my feet up.

When I am in the bathroom, I expect to not be disturbed.
I know I disturb her, but she is not doing anything else.
I whip out my phone and look for a video to watch for twenty minutes.
That should be enough time for me to avoid the majority of the work.
I would prefer to...kick back, lie down and put my feet up.

I hear her walking with purpose outside the door to the bathroom.
I know she is dealing with washing.
I am relieved I am not helping with that.
This video is really interesting about the intricate moves in a video game.
I still prefer to...kick back, lie down and put my feet up.

She calls at me through the bathroom door to say that dinner is ready.
Finally! I can get out and eat something decent.
I reappear in the living room and say "thank you",
So she still feels appreciated.
I deserve to...kick back, lie down and put my feet up.

Dinner is not the best.
She tried something new with cabbage,
I am not a fan.
Only one thing left to do...kick back, lie down
and put my feet up.

Waking Up

I wake up to my wife exuberantly saying, “Wake up!”
I believe that I have now had all the sleep I am allowed.
Night shift is awful when you can't get to sleep after work.
I even got up before she came in the door from work.
With this rude awakening, I already need to...kick back, lie down and put my feet up.

She has generously given me an extra hour in bed.
I am the lucky one!
She has a lot to tell me and I sit up in bed quickly.
I am going to need to concentrate.
I wonder when I can...kick back, lie down and put my feet up.

I get up from bed and she makes me dinner,
Or breakfast in my case.
I then tidy the coffee table,
I have a project to finish.

This is now the time not to think about how I
want to...kick back, lie down and put my feet up.

She looks at me as I place the innards of a
remote control car on the table.
I have left a space for her drink.
I need a new battery,
So I order it for next day delivery.
Nearly time to...kick back, lie down and put my
feet up.

She goes up to bed.
This is my favourite time.
She is not here to complain
Or to give me a job to do.
So I...kick back, lie down and put my feet up.

Staying Out Late

I agreed to spend the day with my friend,
To help fix his car,
And to help him and his son fix a remote control car.
I have fixed up my own car to join in with the fun.
This is no time to...kick back, lie down and put my feet up.

My wife sends me a message telling me what film she is watching,
I ask if it is any good.
She goes into what seems like a university level critique of it.
I really don't care, I was just looking for a yes or no.
She needs to...kick back, lie down and put her feet up.

We need more parts so we have all got in the car to go to mine.
I walk in, she says I am early.
I can see that I have disappointed her when I tell her I have come for more parts.
I leave again.

Why does she not...kick back, lie down and put my feet up.

We have done everything and it is time to go home.
It is 3am and we are supposed to see her Aunt tomorrow.
I know we are leaving at 9:30am.
I am in so much trouble.
Time to...kick back, lie down and put my feet up.

I wake up to her rocking me on the sofa.
I remember thinking this may be the safest place to sleep.
I tell her that I am too tired to go out.
She is rather unhappy.
I just continue to...kick back, lie down and put my feet up.

Unsuccessfully Trying To Redeem Myself

My wife is back from her Aunt's house.
I should have been out with her, but I slept instead.
She has spent 10 hours with her, she must be happy.
I am happy with my own efforts today.
I have stayed...kicked back, laid down with my feet up.

She is ringing the doorbell.
I forgot I put the chain on after the delivery guy arrived.
She is carrying five bags,
I should help.
Afterwards, I know this means I could...kick back, lie down and put my feet up.

I take the bags from her as she gets her coat off.
They are full of clothes, shoes, toiletries and shopping.
Her Aunt has been decluttering again and passing it on to her.
I put away the toiletries and shopping, I have helped.

I know this means I can...kick back, lie down
and put my feet up.

I have left the rest of the bags for her.
I apologise to her again and explain that if I had
gone, I probably would have slept.
She keeps on saying, “OK”, but I really don't
think she is.
I offer to make her a cup of tea, she accepts.
I am closer to...kicking back, laying down and
putting my feet up.

She tells me that washing needs to be put out
and another load done.
I volunteer to do it – later.
She offers to make eggy bread and I say I would
love some.
I say only one slice for me.
When I am eating, I can...kick back, lie down
and put my feet up.

She has burned the egg bread, but I tell her it
tastes good,
It just looks worse than it is.
I ask her where we want to sit and eat it,
I know the importance of trying to make it all up
to her.
Then I can guilt free...kick back, lie down and
put my feet up.

We end up sitting in my lego room, me playing a game while she eats.
It is my suggestion, she looks as if she has begrudgingly agreed.
I state to her that I will do the washing now.
I leave her with the greatest honour, being alone in my room.
I am earning brownie points to...kick back, lie down and put my feet up.

I have managed to get all the washing drying.
I ask her about a pile outside her office, she claims it all needs to go in the wash.
It is time for a delicates wash and I have no idea.
I take the clothes to her that I am unsure about and she confirms they are all delicates.
I am nearly there to...kick back, lie down and put my feet up.

I have done washing now.
I did the washing up earlier,
She has not commented, I am sure I need to get a gold star for my work.
I think it is time to...kick back, lie down and put my feet up.

Sleep Patterns

I did not go to sleep after finishing my final night shift,
I stayed up to repair and improve my radio control cars.
I fell asleep on the sofa later on, when I should have been out with my wife.
She will forgive me, she always does.
I think I will...kick back, lie down and put my feet up.

I went out to spend time with a friend,
I stayed out until 3am.
I fell asleep on the sofa when I got in and did not get up to go out with my wife.
She will forgive me, she always does.
I think I will...kick back, lie down and put my feet up.

I decided to play a video game,
I then decided to catch up on a TV series.
I fell asleep on the sofa and did not get up in time to out with my wife.
She will forgive me, she always does.
I think I will...kick back, lie down and put my feet up.

She tells me that I need to go to bed earlier.
She tells me that I need to get back into a regular
sleeping pattern after night shift.
She tells me that I do this regularly,
After all this hassle from her,
I just go to the sofa and...kick back, lie down
and put my feet up.

Cinema Experience

We have headed to the cinema, we have brought along her brother.
He is my brother from another mother.
I manage to grab a coffee and the reclining seats have been booked.
Even here, I can...kick back, lie down and put my feet up.

I sit next to my bro, we chat and laugh at each others comments.
My wife is at the other side of me insisting I hold her hand.
I suppose it is the least I can do.
With my other hand, I press the button on the chair,
So now I can...kick back, lie down and put my feet up.

Helping The Family

I have agreed to help my bro and my father in law.
My wife also has her own agenda, but that needs to fit in with mine.
She wakes me up, makes me a coffee and we are ready to roll.
We head to my bro's house and we pick up our niece.
Task one complete.
Is it time to...kick back, lie down and put my feet up?

I have dropped my wife and niece at home,
Picked up a few boxes for my father in law,
Items for the recycling centres,
Bags for the charity shop.
Task two complete.
It must be nearly time to...kick back, lie down and put my feet up.

Back to my bro's who has a pile of items for the recycling centre.
We tie part of the sofa to the roof rack,
Everything else can fit inside the car.
The recycling centre receives all of our items.

Task three complete.
I think it is time to...kick back, lie down and put my feet up.

Back to my bro's again to get the next piece of the sofa.
All tied up on the roof rack and ready to go.
The recycling centre watches us struggle to get it in its allocated skip.
We feel victorious.
Task four complete.
It must be time to...kick back, lie down and put my feet up.

We are hungry and require sustenance for our physical efforts.
A quick trip to a shop to get a sandwich.
A quick message to my wife with my spend.
A quick pick up of boxes for my father in law.
Task five complete.
I think it would be most satisfying to...kick back, lie down and put my feet up.

We head to my father in law's.
We hand over the boxes and explain that there are no boxes of the type he is specifically looking for.
We get his long ladder and strap it to the roof rack.

We then attach the high vis jacket to alert other road users.
Task six complete.
I am so close to being able to...kick back, lie down and put my feet up.

We carefully get back to my house.
My niece and wife are waving from the front window.
We unload the ladder and manoeuvre it round the back of the house.
We are met by our ladies outside who want to observe us work.
Task seven complete.
I am unsure, but I believe it is time to...kick back, lie down and put my feet up.

I make my way up the ladder to the gutter.
It is a little windy outside and I am half way up.
It shifts the ladder a little.
I get scared, it is not happening today.
Task eight is for a better weather day.
I am contemplating my next task to be...kicking back, laying down with my feet up.

I head back to my bro's house to unload the rest of the car.
My father in law wanted us to store some cases for him as he moves house next month.

We empty it all into my bro's garage.
We congratulate ourselves on a job well done and get a coffee.
Task nine complete.
I am so close to...kicking back, laying down with my feet up.

We are both feeling good about ourselves.
We have managed so much today.
So we decide to sit down and watch some TV programmes together.
We are awesome.
Task ten complete.
Now we are both...kicked back, laid down with our feet up.

My niece is playing up a little and wants to see daddy.
We head back and she makes a huge welcoming committee for me.
I am the best uncle ever.
Hugs and love are flowing.
Task eleven complete.
I think I will...kick back, lie down and put my feet up.

A few hours later, everyone has left and it is just me and my wife.

I make dinner, she tidies the aftermath of a three year old.
We have both done so much today.
We eat dinner and there is only one more task to complete...kick back, lie down and put my feet up.

Work And The Trainee

The trainee at work has got himself into a situation.
I am far too busy with trials to be able to speak with him.
I am getting help from R&D today.
There are rumours flying about him making an official complaint.
I wish I could find out what is going on
And think about it whilst I...kick back, lie down and put my feet up.

Work has finished and I have a handover.
I find my bro and give him the key to the car.
We give each other the nod of knowing not to get any information from the trainee without the other one being there.
The trainee car shares with us.
It is a longer handover than normal due to the trials.
Soon I will be able to hear what has happened instead of listening to rumours.
Soon I can...kick back, lie down and put my feet up.

I approach the car to find my wife has walked here to get some exercise.
No matter, she can concentrate on driving and I can concentrate on listening.
I am in the car and my bro is straight up with, "tell us what happened with HR."
He tells us everything.
My wife is hooked too and pulls over at a safe place so we can listen more.
We ask questions, the situation is between funny and messed up.
Maybe the trainee highlighted the problem. It may get worse before it gets better.
I long to think about this whilst I...kick back, lie down and put my feet.

Being A Legend To My Wife

My wife is being understanding about me
sleeping at odd times.
She is just letting me snooze when I want.
I think I have a touch of a cold.
I don't know.
She is letting me...kick back, lie down and put
my feet up.

She is not trying to make me do housework.
Housework is boring.
She is, however, trying to rope me into doing
some work.
She needs me to help in her office.
I wonder how much longer I can...kick back, lie
down and put my feet up.

I give it ten minutes, head to her office and she
welcomes me into her sanctuary.
I need a step ladder.
I check the window, it is definitely open at the
top.
I close it. She is happy.
I know I can happily...kick back, lie down and
put my feet up.

She needs me to put up a problematic poster that keeps falling down.
I blow her mind by adding more blue tack to the middle of it.
Six bits. She had never thought of that before.
I am happy to oblige.
I am looking forward to...kicking back, laying down and putting my feet up.

Her vision board is next, it is large.
I want to show interest and ask her questions.
It is good to know what her focus is this year.
I fix it to the wall.
I deserve to...kick back, lie down and put my feet up.

One last job, the calculator is not working.
It is solar powered, but it is nothing to do with the light.
I change the battery, it works.
I am an absolute hero to her tonight.
I feel my legendary status,
Now it's time to...kick back, lie down and put my feet up.

A Helping Hand

I have finished work and my wife has walked
down to the car.
She likes to get some exercise in.
We give the trainee and my bro a lift home.
We swing by a supermarket on the way home so
I can get some beer.
I have run out, then I can open one up and...kick
back, lie down and put my feet up.

We have parked up and she is talking about
something.
I am not listening to her as I see a woman
struggling with her car.
I veer off and ask her if she needs some help.
She says yes and I ask the problem.
She can not open the bonnet, soon I will be able
to...kick back, lie down and put my feet up.

This bonnet is being difficult.
It will definitely not open.
She shows me where it is.
I put a lot of effort into trying to open it,
It is not budging, I wish I was at home to...kick
back, lie down and put my feet up.

As I am working, my wife explains that I am a son of a car mechanic.
They want to know where.
She explains that it is in a different country.
I hope this bonnet opens soon,
I don't want to let her down. Then I can...kick back, lie down and put my feet up.

I finally get it open and I investigate the situation.
It is mechanical and part of the mechanism has seized.
I show her what is happening.
She asks if WD40 would work. I confirm it. She thanks me.
Then she fills the windscreen washer tank, I now need to...kick back, lie down and put my feet up.

I head in to buy my beer.
My wife asks if we have WD40 in the car.
I think we might.
She suggests helping out the woman further if she is still there when we get out.
I agree, then I could get home to...kick back, lie down and put my feet up.

My wife is treating me like a superhero for helping this woman.
She is calling me selfless.

I don't see it that way,
All I did was help someone with skills that I have.
Either way, she is encouraging me to get home, open a beer...kick back, lie down and put my feet up.

www.ingramcontent.com/pod-product-compliance
Lightning Source LLC
Chambersburg PA
CBHW051736130826
49812CB00033B/881
* 9 7 8 9 3 5 7 4 4 0 3 4 9 *